GOA *kids* | GOATS OF ANARCHY

ANGEL
and HER WONDERFUL WHEELS

Brimming with creative inspiration, how-to projects, and useful information to enrich your everyday life, Quarto Knows is a favorite destination for those pursuing their interests and passions. Visit our site and dig deeper with our books into your area of interest: Quarto Creates, Quarto Cooks, Quarto Homes, Quarto Lives, Quarto Drives, Quarto Explores, Quarto Gifts, or Quarto Kids.

Inspiring | Educating | Creating | Entertaining

First Published in 2018 by Walter Foster Jr., an imprint of The Quarto Group.
6 Orchard Road, Suite 100, Lake Forest, CA 92630, USA.
T (949) 380-7510 **F** (949) 380-7575 **www.QuartoKnows.com**

Walter Foster Jr. titles are also available at discount for retail, wholesale, promotional, and bulk purchase. For details, contact the Special Sales Manager by email at specialsales@quarto.com or by mail at The Quarto Group, Attn: Special Sales Manager, 401 Second Avenue North, Suite 310, Minneapolis, MN 55401 USA.

ISBN: 978-1-63322-674-6

Digital edition published in 2018
eISBN: 978-1-63322-675-3

Content development by Saskia Lacey
Illustrated by Jill Howarth

Printed in China
10 9 8 7 6 5 4 3 2 1

GOA kids | GOATS OF ANARCHY

ANGEL
and HER WONDERFUL WHEELS

By **LEANNE LAURICELLA** with Saskia Lacey

Illustrated by **JILL HOWARTH**

One cold night, a young woman found a baby goat lying in a snowy field. The little goat was all alone.

The woman knelt down and gathered the goat in her arms. She noticed the baby goat was hurt and only had two legs.

"Don't worry, little one," she whispered.

The young woman knew the baby goat would need extra love and care. She had heard of a farm that welcomed goats who were sick or hurt and helped them grow strong.

"I know just the place for you," she said, holding the goat close.

She told the little goat all about
the farm. There were other
goats, a pig, chickens, a mini
horse, and a mini donkey. The
goat would have lots of friends
and a mother who would love
her very much.

Her new mother had to drive from far away. When she saw the little goat for the first time, she was filled with love.

"Hi baby," she said. "I'm so happy to meet you!"

The goat slept peacefully during the long ride home. Her new mom decided to name her Angel. It was the name of the kind young woman who had saved the baby goat.

When Angel arrived at her new home,
she was greeted by Piney the pig. He lived
in the house and was sweet and friendly.

During her first days at the farm, Angel's
mom carried the baby goat everywhere.

Sometimes, Angel's mom laid the little goat next to the window. Angel stared curiously at the animals outside.

Angel was happy, but her mom wanted to help the baby goat learn how to move around on her own.

Angel's mom had never cared for a goat like Angel. She wanted more than anything to help the little goat walk. Angel's mom prayed that she would find the right answer.

One day, she saw a picture in a magazine of a dog using a cart to walk. It was the perfect solution for Angel!

When a big brown box arrived in the mail, the little goat and her mom opened it together. Angel was so excited. She couldn't wait to see the cart.

It was pink! Carefully, Angel's mom placed the baby goat in the cart.

Angel tried to pull the cart, but it wouldn't budge. She pulled harder. One wheel creaked forward—but then it stopped. Angel sighed and looked up at her mom and Piney.

"Keep going," her mom urged. "You can do this." Piney gave Angel an encouraging nudge.

Even though it was hard, Angel tried again and again. The little goat pulled with all her strength. Slowly, the cart inched forward. Angel took one step, and then another. The baby goat was walking on her own!

With practice, Angel walked faster and faster. Eventually, the little goat was happily running from one end of the house to the other. Angel's mom knew that her prayers had been answered.

Soon after Angel got her cart, another baby goat moved into the house. He wore two bright blue braces on his front legs.

"Hi, I'm Angel," she said with a bashful smile.

"Hi, Angel. I'm Miles!" The baby goat hopped around Angel.

Miles had *a lot* of energy. He wanted to know all about the little pink cart. Angel told him that the cart helped her walk, run, and spin. Miles said his blue braces helped him run and bounce!

Angel and Miles became best friends
even though they were very different.
Angel was a serious and determined
little goat, while Miles was energetic
and goofy.

As they explored the house, Angel trotted in her cart and Miles bounced alongside. Sometimes, the two friends pretended to be super goats! Angel sped around the house, zooming this way and that. Miles bounced off of everything, even Piney!

One day, Piney took Angel and Miles outside to meet the other goats. Angel noticed that one of the goats only had three legs. But none of them had a cart like hers. She felt embarrassed. Why was she the only one with a cart?

One by one, the goats came up to say hello. Some were curious, but others looked nervous. They had never seen anything like Angel's pink cart.

A few of the goats encouraged Angel to show them what her cart could do. But Angel was scared to walk in front of the goats. What if they laughed?

Angel stomped her hoof. She wasn't going to be scared! Slowly, she began to walk. As she moved forward, Miles and Piney cheered. Angel walked faster and faster until she was running. The other goats pranced excitedly.

Angel spun in circles, zooming all over the farm while the other goats watched in amazement. Miles bounced up and down. Everyone loved her little pink cart!

That night, Angel sighed as she cuddled by the fire with Miles and Piney. At first, meeting the older goats had been scary. But Angel had shown the other goats that she could run just like them.

As she settled into the blankets, the baby goat smiled. Angel was happy and very proud.

As time passed, more baby goats came to live at the farm. Some had trouble walking. Angel welcomed these little goats. She understood how it felt to be new and a bit different.

Angel helped the baby goats as they learned to use their carts. She cheered when they ran for the first time!

Angel loved her new life. Each day at the farm was filled with excitement and adventure. Angel couldn't wait to see where her wonderful wheels would take her next!

The End

ANGEL
and HER WONDERFUL WHEELS

The True Story

Hi, I'm Leanne Lauricella. People also call me "Goat Mama" because I rescue baby goats. I have a farm called Goats of Anarchy in New Jersey, where I care for more than 80 goats. Plus, we also take care of 8 sheep, 2 pigs, 6 horses, 6 dogs, chickens, alpacas, 3 miniature horses, and a miniature donkey. We have a very full house!

Leanne

Angel

This is Angel. She is a little black and white fainting goat. Goats like Angel actually faint when they get surprised!

Poor little Angel was born out in the snow when she was a baby. It was so cold that she got frostbite and lost her back legs and the tips of her ears.

She was so tiny and frail when she first came to me. I nursed her wounds and placed her in bed next to Piney. There was an instant connection between them. They were like old friends!

Piney would curl up around Angel in a "pig hug." And Angel would lean on Piney and groom his hair! It was the start of a very sweet friendship.

Angel and Piney

We wanted to get Angel up and moving, so I found a sweet little pink cart to help her get around. The first time I put Angel in the cart, she gave me a look that said, "No way!" She wouldn't move. Not one step.

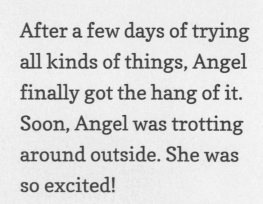

After a few days of trying all kinds of things, Angel finally got the hang of it. Soon, Angel was trotting around outside. She was so excited!

After Angel got her cart, she made friends with Miles, another goat who needed help walking. These two were inseparable!

Angel and Miles

Angel didn't have a goat mom to teach her how to eat hay, so it was hard to get her to eat. I tried everything and nothing worked, until I made her a hay smoothie— she loved that!

Angel has grown quite a bit since she first came to our farm. She is lovable and feisty, and stubborn as ever.

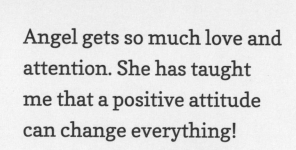

Angel gets so much love and attention. She has taught me that a positive attitude can change everything!